TERREN

Contributions by
Jim McGregor & Marilyn Mitchell

To Roxy
You are the greatest
with gratitude

Terence Morrissey

THE FINAL DIVE

The Final Dive
Copyright © 2016 by Terrence Morrissey

This book and/or any parts thereof, including pictures and inserted copied letters, etc., may not be reproduced in any form, stored in any retrieval system, or transmitted in any form by any means including, but not limited to, electronic, mechanical, photocopy, recording, or otherwise – without the prior written permission of the author or his assigns. All pictures and letters are legally copyrighted material and are the sole property of the author.

Tellwell Talent
www.tellwell.ca

ISBN
978-1-77302-150-8 (Paperback)
978-1-77302-151-5 (eBook)

INTRODUCTION

A chance meeting with one of the most popular and powerful men in the world led this young businessman on a boating and spearfishing trip that eventually, because of the simple words uttered by Robert Kennedy, changed this young man's life forever. This change came about many years after the "Final Dive" with Mr. Kennedy. Read about a 'spear fishing' trip, late dinners and some 'night clubbing' in the Bahamas and "The Miracle on Kalakaua Avenue" in Waikiki.

This story, although short, speaks volumes, in its simplicity, of the wonderment of a great man as seen through my eyes. I have often wondered, as have others, just how much greater the wonderful country called The United States of America would have been had Bobby lived out his dream of becoming the President and likewise had his brother John lived. We will never know but in our collective hearts we somehow know that it would have been infinitely better.

Bobby was one of the kindest men I have ever met. I realize my association with him was very short and so my assessment might leave a question mark in many people's minds….and rightfully so. On what do I base my opinion, one might ask? Simply something I read a long time ago in a very popular book that has proven itself to be accurate on every occasion….."The eyes are the mirror of the soul and out of the abundance of the heart the mouth speaks." Using this formula and being an observant and relatively intelligent human being I am confident my assessment of Bobby is accurate… He, Bobby, was one of the kindest and most loving human being I have ever had the honor of meeting, sharing with and shaking hands with.

United States Senate
WASHINGTON, D.C.

November 18, 1966

Dear Mr. Morrissey:

I just wanted you to know how much I appreciated everything you did for us during our recent trip to Nassau. You were very thoughtful to give of your time -- and to be so helpful in so many ways.

I hope that someday Mrs. Kennedy and I shall have an opportunity to see you again. In the meantime, many thanks, and our warm regards,

Sincerely,

My Thanks to you
[signature]

Robert F. /Kennedy

Mr. Terrance Morrissey
Hertz Corporation
Post Office Box 558
Nassau, THE BAHAMAS

DEDICATION

I want to dedicate this book to all the folks that were helpful and supportive of what I have attempted to accomplish….and that is to just tell my story with the hopeful anticipation that somewhere, somehow someone, no matter who you are or where you are or what you are going through, you are never alone and you are a precious and valuable human being who is very much loved.

If I neglect to thank the following folks I will be all the sadder for having missed a wonderful opportunity to 'Shout it out" and publically declare my sincere appreciation for your love, compassion and understanding of me as a person with some faults and defects but a man who has always wished he could 'do it over'. But life is what it is and the following folks have loved me through some pretty painful times and for that I will be eternally grateful.

Jim McGregor, a friend who has shown such incredible patience as I spent so much time requesting his assistance, not only with this book, but with things in life that sometimes plagued me. Jim is a man of distinction who, as a writer like myself, deserves much, much more than I can offer him. But I can introduce you all to Jim by asking you to go 'on line' and check out the poem, titled "Climb Higher" that Jim wrote and now occupies a permanent place at the World Trade Center catastrophe, honoring the heroes, who were willing to sacrifice their lives in order that others might live.

Marilyn Mitchell, you bless me with your kindness, patience and caring heart. How God must rejoice in your love of others and how, through your nursing career, you have helped heal many a wounded man and woman. Thanks for helping with the manuscript…. your suggestions have been extremely valuable. I am grateful to you.

Terrence

THE FINAL DIVE
Spearfishing in the Bahamas

It was late in 1966 that I read in the local newspaper that Robert Kennedy was visiting Nassau in the Bahamas and was staying at Lyford Cay. As the manager of a car rental company I decided to ask Mr. Kennedy if I could put a car at his disposal while he visited. Mr. Kennedy's aide called me a day later and said that Mr. Kennedy would like to accept the offer. Rather than have one of my employees deliver the car I delivered it myself to Mr. Kennedy at Lyford Cay for the simple reason that I would like to meet the man I so much admired. What you are about to read is a true story. I hope you enjoy reading the story as much as the joy I had, in most cases, living it. Bobby and I dined, went night clubbing had a B-B-Q at his residence along with some of his friends and most of all we went Spear Fishing in the waters off of Nassau in the beautiful Bahamas. While talking with Bobby, as we were walking on the beach one evening, he made a suggestion that some years later would change my life completely and forever.

The drive was slow. Not because of traffic, because there was none. It was the excitement I was feeling as I thought of my destination. The surrounding beauty warped time out of perspective and into slow motion. The sun was setting off in the western sky. A crimson yellow and red, as beautiful a sunset as can be seen anywhere in the world. Water stretching to the horizon, as vast as the eye could see and the sun starting to dip beyond the horizon. The red, yellow and crimson of the sky took my breath away. I see the sunset every day as I see the sunrise in the morning but I never tire of looking at it. It is a painted canvas as no man could paint; only the painting Gods of heaven could create such a masterpiece.

I was the only car on the road as far as the eye could see. The winding road covered in places with drifting sand, could be treacherous. Cruising along while glancing at the vast ocean I caught sight of a ship, outlined against the fading daylight, about a quarter of a mile off shore, as it made its way into the Nassau harbor; this was always a time of dreaming and wondering. Where did she come from, what was her final destination and what was she carrying? Questions without answers but I didn't really need answers at a time like this. I was dreaming and driving in the beautiful Bahamas and truly, at this time in my life absolutely nothing really mattered as I was thinking that nothing is more beautiful than the Beautiful Bahamas, so aptly named.

A little further down the road and around another bend I could see the luxury yachts plying their way into Nassau Harbor. Tourists, locals or visiting strangers from far off places, returning from a day of deep sea fishing or maybe some snorkeling with a little treasure hunting thrown in. I have experienced it all, but now I was driving to an experience that, unbeknownst to me at that moment, would occupy my thoughts from time to time for the rest of my life.

The times were tranquil; we hadn't yet reached the point in time of police boarding's of yachts, of both the innocent and the guilty. Neither had we reached the time whereby drugs, murder and shootouts would be taking place on the high seas in vastly increased numbers in many of these waters. Those days were yet to come. These were the good times and the people of the Bahamas were happy and free spirited. Only when drugs started to flow in large quantities did serious mistrust appear and anxiety start to raise its ugly head. Soon to be gone would be these days when whether you are white, black or any color in between you could have one too many at a local bar and know that if you passed out, when you awoke your wallet and its contents would still be in your pocket. But for now, bliss and joy held my life in their hands.

These are the times I was living in, times of peace, brotherhood and tranquility, and I loved every moment of it. That is why the drive was slow; there just was no hurry to get anywhere. I was on my way to meet one of the most powerful men in the world. With more power and more friends in high places than most people, not only in America, but in almost every country of the world.

I was cruising as if I was on a Sunday afternoon drive with my wife and kids. Sure, the excitement was there at the prospects of what this meeting would bring, but 'hurry' seemed to have vacated my vocabulary and life style.

I turned off the sand-blown road and made my way between two rows of trees. They formed a canopy that shaded me with a welcome coolness as I squinted through the dancing shadows, seeking the small building at the end of the road. Then suddenly it was there, looming out of the shadows. A black police officer in the standard sparkling white uniform with gold braids, signifying seniority, stood at attention on my left, as I approached the gated property. Two other men, one white and one black, were standing off to my right, dressed in business suits. I knew they were hot under the Bahamian sun and no doubt uncomfortable in those 'Washington' suits.

I swallowed hard; they did not know me and I wondered what kind of reception awaited me. I wondered if I had my wallet in my back pocket, and, as I reached around to check, I noticed that the white man in the business suit squinted his eyes curiously and reached inside his jacket. He held his hand there, in a kind of nonchalant manner. I slowed the convertible to a crawl and approached the gate.

There was a guard hut on my left, large enough to hold two people, a desk, telephone and a small refrigerator. It was painted yellow with a light brown door. The trim around the facade was also painted a clean clear light brown. A smartly dressed uniformed guard stepped out and approached the car. I sweated a little as I wondered what type of questions he was going to ask. What was I going to say? "Oh, I'm here to see the next President of the United States" and the gate would swing open and with a slight bow the guard would smile and say, "Go right straight in, Mr. Morrissey, Mr. Kennedy is waiting to see you"?

Well, you could have knocked me over with a feather. As I pulled up alongside the guard shack, the guard stepped up to the car, the convertible top was down and the smartly dressed guard with a no-nonsense smile on his face looked at me and said, "Good afternoon, sir, go right on ahead, Mr. Kennedy is expecting you."

It was only later on that I discovered that when a Kennedy is present, no one, but no one, who is not well known to all of the security people, enters their compound, be it at Hyannis Port, Washington, or Lyford Cay, in the Bahamas.

The guard on the gate, well, it just so happened that he too was an FBI agent but dressed in the standard uniform of a guard at a traffic gate. The regular guard was given a few days off, with pay, and told to enjoy himself.

I found out later that the Kennedy staff or FBI had done a background check on me long before I was to meet Robert Kennedy and at that point knew things about me that I myself had forgotten years ago.

All security was doubled as a result of Robert's brother, President Jack Kennedy's, assassination in the not too distant past. The world was soon to witness, shortly after this trip, Robert Kennedy's last Bahamian vacation, that he, too, regardless of security, would be gunned down.

"Straight ahead and at the 'T,' make a left turn, Mr. Morrissey, and Mr. Kennedy will be in the first cottage on your left", the man in gold directed as I let my eyes wander over the so called "Cottages."

To me they looked like little mansions, nicer than many homes I had seen in upscale neighborhoods. Small, relatively speaking, yes, but everything about this place from the personally designed 'cottages' to the luxurious and well-manicured lawns, gardens and the splendid tennis courts, shouted 'wealth' and I sensed a comfortable but friendly wealth.

Pulling up in the driveway of the first cottage on my left, I almost wanted to turn around and leave. This was a breathtaking moment for me and I was overwhelmed by what would be the enormity of the meeting with Robert F. Kennedy, the brother of the past President of the United States of America and, just possibly, the next President of the United States. I got out of the car, a 1966 fire engine red Impala convertible with white upholstery. I enjoyed the attention I received as I drove my block-long convertible down Bay Street in downtown Nassau and along the very narrow back streets. It got me plenty of attention and, during the future elections of 1969 when Mr. Pindeling's Bahamian Party was ahead in the polls, this same car got the kind of attention that I could have done without. Pindeling, a black Bahamian, was in, and the white British, who had held a tight rein on the Bahamian people and the Bahamas for almost three hundred and fifty years, were out. I was Canadian, but to the Bahamians, if I was white, I was British. I realized the seriousness of the election and the fervor of the people when one day I was at a stop sign at a street corner when out of nowhere, to my surprise, I was splattered with black ink. The white upholstery of my convertible also took a bath. I still love the Bahamian people to this day and I understand the emotions of the time.

"Hi," spoke a voice from the patio, and as the speaker swiveled in his chair to face me I was staring into the smiling face and smiling eyes of Robert

Kennedy. "Pull up a chair and make yourself comfortable" he said as he stood and walked over and shook my hand. "I'm Robert and this is Mr. Billings." He then introduced two other gentlemen and the wife of one of his friends. After introducing myself to everyone, I moved in and made myself comfortable in a lawn chair.

"Drink?" Mr. Kennedy asked. "Don't mind if I do, it sure is a sweltering day today", I offered in the way of small conversation. Mr. Kennedy looked at me with a quizzical look in his eye and said, "You must be used to the weather, you live here in Nassau permanently". "I am used to it, Mr. Kennedy", I offered, "but there are days, such as this one, whereby the humidity becomes so high that it is just hard on everyone, including the people who live here, the Bahamians."

"Terry", Mr. Kennedy spoke with softness and a twinkle in his eye, but with certain seriousness, "Please, just call me Robert. I can be Mr. Kennedy everywhere else but here in Nassau even Mr. Billings calls me Robert." At that comment, everyone laughed. I was to find out later that Mr. Billings was Robert's friend from childhood, well, at least from his college days. The ice was broken and everyone relaxed, including me, as I asked for a rum and coke; what other drink would I drink when I lived, laughed and partied in the Bahamas!

After some general conversation about the Bahamas, the weather and the style of living in Nassau, peppered with a few questions about my hobbies and some well-placed humor from Mr. Kennedy and Mr. Billings as they bantered back and forth, I decided it was time to leave.

Downing my third rum and coke I addressed Mr. Kennedy;

"Well, Mr. Kennedy, ooops Robert," I corrected myself, "I had better be getting on back to downtown Nassau. I have quite a few items still to take care of and my wife will be anxious to hear all about our meeting." I was attempting to not overstay my welcome, as I was sure he, Robert, had a zillion things to do that would be of vastly more importance than chatting with me. While it felt awkward to be addressing him by his first name, the awkwardness only lasted for a short while as he knew exactly how to make a stranger feel at home and very comfortable.

"Listen," Robert said, "I'll drive you back in myself. I like the car you have, and as we are short of transportation maybe I can borrow yours." This man has class, I thought to myself. Here he was, making like he wanted to borrow my car when all the while the reason I was out there was to lend it to him for his vacation. It was an arrangement I had made two days earlier with Mr. Billings and one of the FBI agents. "Sounds good to me", I said.

I drove and Robert sat in the front with me. He asked lots of questions about the Island, the people, poverty, freedom of movement, free enterprise, etc., etc. Robert had a way of asking questions that made you feel you were part of a conversation and not just a source of information. We were bonding, and I could feel that he liked me; I would have no trouble relating to him or communicating with him in any manner. In fact by the time we reached the Pilot House club on Bay Street, I felt a real kinship with this man. I am not sure exactly how to describe it, but I felt as if I had known him for a great many years.

"Terry, what about some fishing and how about dinner tomorrow night?" I was amazed at the invitation, but I was delighted also. "How about some spear fishing?" I offered. "Wow, Robert exclaimed, "Now that sounds good. Do you have any experience?" he queried? I replied, with some degree of pride, that I happened to be the president of a spear fishing club here in Nassau called the Nassau Sea Hunters. "I also spear fished in the Virgin Islands and Puerto Rico", I offered

Billings asked, "Robert, don't you remember the article in the paper that we saw yesterday about Terry and his "Nassau Sea Hunters?". Billings reached into his coat pocket and shuffling some papers he began to read from the newspaper article …."The Bahamas is to have its first official spearfishing club…The Nassau Sea Hunters." Billings continued to read from the newspaper article…. Mr. Terry Morrissey, president of the Nassau Sea Hunters, said the Ministry of Tourism has expressed its enthusiasm in the new venture and the ministry of Agriculture and Fisheries has also shown an interest." (The article appeared in the Nassau Sunday Guardian on July 17, 1966). Robert replied, "Oh, yes now I recall and wasn't there another story about an incident at a swimming pool and some child almost drowning?"

Now it was my turn to ask a question.

"How did you know about that? The article about the Sea Hunters and that incident at the swimming pool happened months ago". The other gentleman in the back spoke up, "You don't think that you are here without us having checked on you, do you?" I was surprised, because I never thought for a minute that I was worth checking on and I expressed that view. "Well, we probably know more about you than you think. We even check the newspapers to see if your name shows up in any articles. You can understand the necessity of these actions," he continued, "if we are to safeguard Mr. Kennedy who could possibly be the next president of the United States."

"You make a lot of sense", I said, "I just never gave it any thought." "OK; spear fishing tomorrow along with some scuba. I will pick you all up at 8:00 am and we can get an early start and beat the heat of the afternoon sun. We'll hunt up some Bahamian lobster and have us a good old-fashioned cook-out." As we were driving back to my house, Robert exclaimed, "Terry, you're a man after my own heart." "Hey," Billings yelled from the back seat, "why not have Terry join us for dinner tonight and we can plan the excursion?" "OK with you, Terry?" Robert asked. "What time and where?" I replied. "Our place at Lyford Cay", Billings was yelling against the wind as my foot, in all this excitement, was heavy on the gas pedal. "I'll be there, say about 7:00.

That evening after dinner was over and what an incredible dinner it was a dinner of steak, vegetables and lobster served with a side of black- eyed peas and rice, I found myself walking the beach with Robert Kennedy and sharing a conversation that primarily touched on generalities, and every once in a while the conversation would slip into somewhat personal talk about home life, families, relationships with other people.

One thing that stood out was Robert's obvious concern and love for others. He frequently talked about our responsibilities to others and how it was our duty to always seek out and help others wherever and whenever it was possible and there was a need. His compassion for all fellow humans was blatantly obvious and very touching. Robert struck me as a very sensitive person who, if he had a magic wand, would wave it across the earth and make all things right for the less fortunate peoples who suffer great pain and tragedy on a daily basis.

The sun was starting to set in the western sky, it was getting late. Robert turned to me and was asking me a question. "So Terry, tell me how are the conditions for the black people here in Nassau? What I mean is, how is their standard of living? The ones I have met seem to be very happy and very relaxed." I answered, "Well, I have been here for almost three years and I just love these folks. They are generous to a fault. Their attitude towards us white folks is extraordinary. This is their home, their Island, and they welcome all visitors, regardless of their race or color, with respect, and always with a big 'welcome to my Island' attitude". Robert and I walked and talked, as we had been doing for the past hour and a half, along the beach at Lyford Cay, always looking out to sea and admiring everything along the way.

"Regarding your questions about their standard of living, there are times that I feel the business owners could step up to the plate and pay a few dollars more in salaries and pay a few dollars more for services that the Bahamian people provide. Over all, though, the people enjoy a fairly good and decent living. Certainly, there are those Bahamians that are very wealthy and then at the other end of the scale there are the very poor.

In between, you have the middle class." Robert cut in at this point and offered that the situation sounds pretty much like home. "We seem to have parallel cultures whereby we have the wealthy, the middle class and the poor in both America and Canada where you are from, Terry, and also in the Bahamas."

"Right, Robert", I countered, "there are certainly similarities, with one major exception". Robert cut in,

"What would that be?" I paused, took a deep breath and said, "Robert, just look around you, tell me where in the world would we find such beauty and not only the beauty of the elements, the crimson sky, the soft rainfalls every once in a while, the luxurious foliage, the incredible array of flowers, and to be greeted each day with a sunrise beautiful enough to knock your socks off?" Robert laughed and replied, "Right you are, Terry, right you are. It is an honor to be invited into the home and Island of these wonderful people."

I left Lyford Cay with a light step and a happy heart. It was inspiring to have chatted with Mr. Kennedy and to know that even people in such high positions could have so much love and concern for others. His love for his family knew no bounds. He spoke about them often and in such detail, describing how each one of his children just filled his heart with happiness and joy. His love for his wife was obvious in just the little references he made about her and the softness with which he spoke whenever he mentioned her name. My imagination? Possibly, but that is the way I felt as he talked.

As I drove away from Lyford Cay and that meeting with Robert, my mind started to wander backwards, and in a trance-like driving state that overcomes us once in a while I thought of just a few days before my first meeting with Robert Kennedy and how I almost missed one of the great opportunities of a lifetime that comes along very, very rarely; how I almost blew this whole adventure because I was an alcoholic and the booze took over and replaced rational thinking with that sick 'just one more drink', thinking.

I was being paged….

…."Paging Mr. Morrissey, paging Mr. Morrissey." I could hear the words that sounded so far off in the distance of my mind. It was as though the sound was coming from outer space, the sound travelling the distance from the speaker to my mind in what seemed like an eternity. The sound came closer, became louder. "Paging Mr. Morrissey, paging Mr. Morrissey" it repeated over and over.

Fear, shock, and surprise overtook me as I opened my eyes and realized I was being paged. I was sleeping on the floor in one of the rooms of the Pilot House Hotel on Bay Street in Nassau, which was located across from the boat harbor. "Good grief, what time is it?" I was thinking as I fumbled around for my watch; I found it, and the time on the watch said seven thirty. Seven thirty? I was trying to clear the cobwebs out of my head; was it seven thirty at night or seven thirty in the morning?

I was panicking, my heart was racing and I was confused. Then it occurred to me. I was supposed to pick up Bobby Kennedy and his friends at Lyford Cay to go spear fishing. Reaching for the phone, I dialed "O", and the hotel operator said, "Good Morning, Mr. Morrissey. Gardner is trying to reach you."

"Get him on the phone for me" I mumbled. A few rings, and Gardner's voice came over the line. "Terry, where the hell are you? We were supposed to meet at seven fifteen and I have the boat all ready for the spear fishing trip with Kennedy". "I'm across the street from you", I answered. "I spent the night in the hotel so I could get going early in the morning to pick up Kennedy, but I overslept. I sure am glad you called. Listen Gardner", I continued, "do me a favor and call Lyford Cay tell them I will be about fifteen minutes late. I am getting dressed right now and heading out the door." There was a long pause and I could hear Gardner taking a deep breath before he answered "OK, but get going; I have cancelled all my charters for today and tomorrow to accommodate you". I said, "Thanks Gardner, I'm on my way."

What a mess! I stumbled around trying to get my legs into my pants, and after a search I found my shirt. I was out the door and stopped in the hallway at the top of the stairs to put on my shoes. At the bottom of the stairs were the kitchen and the bar. I made my way through the kitchen and asked for a cup of hot coffee, double cream and double sugar. Without stopping, I stepped into the bar through the swinging doors and spotted Fergie, the bartender, setting up for the day's business. "Ferguson" I shouted, "Give me straight scotch. Don't ask any questions and don't talk to me" I concluded.

Fergie scooted behind the deserted bar and poured me a drink. I gulped it down, and on my way out I yelled back "I'll pay you later". I looked at Fergie to see his reaction and all I saw was a big grin, and the words that followed that grin were, "You sure look like hell, Mr. Morrissey". "See you later", I replied and I was back out through the swinging doors, grabbed my coffee and said, "Put it on the tab". I reached my vehicle that was parked in front of the hotel, jumped into the driver's seat and was off like a shot heading for Lyford Cay.

While driving, I was thinking about Lyford Cay and its beauty. Lyford Cay was developed and built to cater to the lifestyles of the rich and the famous. It was developed with a very high regard for privacy and security. There are those that enjoy a style of life that demands the highest quality in all things and that includes safety and security. Many aspire to this lifestyle, including me, but few, again including me, ever reach that plateau.

Lyford Cay is located on the Western end of New Providence Island, which is always referred to as Nassau. Nassau is actually a city on the Island of New Providence. Gate-guarded security is highly maintained at Lyford Cay, because all who reside there, whether permanently or for a week, month or six months a year, demand and feel entitled to it. Some, because of their standing in the community or the worldwide community, require it. Lyford Cay is a thousand acres of very natural beauty, and is home to some of the world's most beautiful beaches and crystal-clear waters.

Lyford Cay is safe, friendly and peaceful, and a lot of the residents that live there travel around in their golf carts. It also has a leading primary and junior school and has its own Lyford Cay Hospital. Membership in the exclusive Club is optional and provides, as one would expect, a very high level of service, confidentiality and security. Membership also includes the use of an 18-hole championship golf course, meticulously maintained. There are also tennis courts and a yacht harbor with formal and informal dining and included are guest houses and cottages.

Pulling into Lyford Cay, I was once again greeted at the Security guard house by the affable and always aware security guard. "Good morning, Mr. Morrissey", he spoke, and then continued, "Go right on in. Mr. Kennedy is expecting you". "Thank you", I shot back and headed the seven-passenger van, which I had commandeered the night before, in the direction of the Kennedy house.

Stopping the car in front of the lawn and the walkway that led to the main entrance, I got out and started toward the front door. I was only a few feet into the short journey when a voice rang out "Good morning, Terry". It was Billings, the family friend. He walked toward me and, extending his hand, he continued, "It is good to see you again. Robert will be right down. He had a few last minute calls to make". "Sorry I'm late", I started to explain, but I was interrupted by Billings with, "Don't you worry about it. The timing is perfect, as we all had a few last minute things to take care of". Bobby came out of the house. "Good morning", he said with that big old friendly smile of his. "Everyone ready to go"? He continued. "We sure are", enthusiastically rang out the chorus of the six of us. I am not sure who the other two men were but they were introduced as friends of the family, one by the name of Rodney and the other's name was James. Both very friendly, and by the alert look in their eyes I was pretty well convinced that I was taking a couple of FBI agents spear fishing.

"Everyone in and belted?" I asked. Affirmative responses all around, although I noticed that two of my guests did not have seat belts hooked up. "OK, we're off to do some really neat spear fishing" I offered as we headed out of Lyford Cay and into Nassau and the Yacht Harbor. "This island is a paradise", spoke James. "It sure is", replied his sidekick. Billings offered that Nassau has a long history and very close ties with the United Sates but even closer ties to England as The Bahamas had been under British rule in 1966 for approximately three hundred years.

We all offered bits of information about the Bahamas; fishing, boating, and the night life and always without hesitation were the comments about how friendly the Bahamian people are.

Nassau is New Providence's main city and the capital of the Bahamas. The city has a long and varied history of charm, style and tourism, and it was to become busy and industrious in the not too distant future, embracing communication and financial services.

In Nassau one can find colonial-style buildings, museums and art galleries. The highlight of each year is the annual holiday known as 'Junkanoo'. The origin of the word 'Junkanoo' is said to be from the name John Canoe, an African prince and slave trader operating off the Gold Coast in the seventeenth century. To the slaves, he was a hero and he was worshipped and idolized by them. Junkanoo is celebrated with parades on December 26 and on New Year's Day right smack down the center of Nassau on the main street, known as Bay Street. Both locals and tourists alike get involved, and there is a great deal of what I like to call 'Good old- fashioned Bahamian partying'.

There would be so much more to Nassau in future years as opposed to the quiet tranquil little paradise that we were presently enjoying. There would be a world-class water park and incredibly beautiful and playable golf courses. A destination for cruise ships because of its superior shopping advantages with cameras, crystal and electronics dominating the market place. Then there is the 'Straw Market'. Aptly named because one can buy almost anything that can be made from straw, this is a great hit with the tourists. We won't want to forget about the casinos, Crystal Palace on Cable Beach, and the Atlantis Casino on Paradise Island

Pulling up before the Nassau Yacht Harbor on Bay Street and cruising into the parking lot, we were greeted by my good friend and one of the most celebrated individuals in the diving, snorkeling, spear fishing, scuba diving, and treasure and shark hunters in the world, and a celebrity in the Bahamas, Gardner Young. A legend in his lifetime, Gardner had been the guiding force that kept many movie stars, extras and directors alive with his knowledge of the undersea world of the Bahamas. He was the most sought-after individual on the Island when it came to anything connected with diving and underwater safety, but, most of all, staying alive.

"Good morning, Terry". I could see the 'where the hell have you been?' look in his eyes as we shook hands. I introduced Gardner to everyone and then we headed for Gardner's charter boat.

It was specially equipped for charter diving for both tourists and professionals alike. Well equipped with everything from spear fishing equipment, cameras, food, drinks of all kinds and plenty of hot coffee.

Stepping aboard, we were greeted by expert diver, Sam Cancilla, a native Canadian who, although employed elsewhere on the Island, was more at home in the water than on land. Sam was an entertainer and my very best friend. Sam extended his warm friendly hand to all in the party and then, looking at me again with that 'where the hell have you been?' look, he started to pour drinks all around.

Mr. Kennedy and two members of his entourage drank Bloody Marys' out of a coffee cup. Robert explained to me that this was in order that should anyone be close enough to take a picture it would appear as if they were drinking coffee.

As for me, a long Bloody Mary in a tall plastic glass was perfectly suitable. Sam went on to explain, while he expertly mixed the Bloody Marys' that the drink was created by George Jessel in 1939. Sam, my buddy and a fountain of knowledge, held our attention while he further explained that George Jessel was a singer, songwriter and also an academy award winning movie producer.

"Tell us more", chimed in Billings when Sam started to lose interest in the topic. "Well", Sam went on, "about Mr. Jessel, George was also a multitalented comedic entertainer and was known by his nickname 'The Toastmaster General of the United States.'"

"How did he acquire that title?" asked Gardner. "He was tagged with it by someone at a ceremony because of George's role as the Master of Ceremonies at entertainment and political gatherings." At that, we all raised our glasses and coffee cups and saluted Sam. I should mention that my good friend Sam Cancilla has the keenest mind of any man I have ever known and he has stored up a vast amount of knowledge on many subjects.

The trip was discussed, and Gardner, after assessing everyone's capabilities, likes and dislikes, fears and expectations, explained all the rules of diving. They were simple, with heavy emphasis on safety. Gardner was one of the first charter boat captains to install underwater cameras on his boat that would allow him or a mate to monitor all the divers as they played and spear fished in the water beneath the boat. The cameras were expensive and had a far reach. The crystal-clear waters of the Bahamas certainly helped with clarity and distance. Each party of four divers had to have an experienced certified diver along for safety. As I was certified and a veteran diver, I was allowed the privilege of monitoring the party that swam with me. This consisted of Robert Kennedy, Billings, one FBI security, and my best friend on the Island, Sam Cancilla.

Before hitting the water I asked for everyone's attention. The joking and chatter came to a halt as all eyes turned toward me. "I just want to take a minute or two to explain a few things about what we are about to engage in and this is for the folks on board who might appreciate the information about spear fishing if it is all new to them and also this should be a reminder to all of us, myself included, about the seriousness of what we are about to undertake as a reminder that "SAFETY" (and I emphasized the word) comes first at all times... someone's life might hang in the balance of being aware or not being aware of the dangers that await us. Is it safe? You might ask, of course it is safe... but it is wise to remember that there are predators in these waters that, if given a chance, could kill a diver in an instant."

With that last sentence I had all of their attention immediately....looking over at Gardner I noticed a smile on his face...Gardner knew that this was necessary and he also knew, due to our long spear fishing adventures that I was a very 'safety conscious' person. A few minutes now may save a life, a serious injury or future grief.

I continued...."We are going hunting. You are going to use skills that some of you never even realized that you had. You will see much 'game' in these waters and you must decide which to focus on. You will have to, just like hunting big game in Africa, stalk your game, hunt it with skill and make a kill." I heard a deep sigh and someone asked, "Do we have all the gear that we need for this hunt?" "Yes, you are being furnished with all the appropriate gear. You have been issued a mask, a spear gun, a snorkel and as a precaution you have been issued a knife." I turned the session over to Gardner and he took a short time to explain things like buoyancy, spear gun safety, and explained the type of reefs we would be diving on and what to watch for. Someone asked "What is the knife for?"

Gardner explained that the knife has many uses. "A knife, Gardner explained, has many uses one of which is to kill your catch as humanely as possible and no, that is not bad, this is just good fishing whether on land or under the water." He continued. "The knife is also used if there is entanglement and you or someone else gets tangled in weeds, they can be cut free. The most important aspect, which, by the way, is extremely rare, is for self-protection." He continued, as he saw the fear on one person's face, "Don't be alarmed, I have dived in these waters with Terry for many, many years and we have NEVER had to use the knife for protection….we see danger, we avoid it by just getting out of the water and finding another spot to spear fish." Now, Gardner said, with a wide grin, "let's get into this water and have a whale of a time!"

Then he added "No there are no whales nearby." With laughter and calmness restored we headed over the side of the dive boat and into the undersea waters of the beautiful Bahamas. Then the fun began.

Serious diving but fun nonetheless. Everyone did an excellent job of adhering to the safety rules as outlined and everyone was an accomplished swimmer. Robert Kennedy was especially good and I noticed during our dive and our spear fishing that he was competitively aggressive in a friendly but determined manner. He was a joy to dive with as his sense of 'what to do next' was excellent.

We spent about three hours of free diving, spear fishing and snorkeling. Due to strict regulations in the Bahamas regarding spear fishing and the use of SCUBA gear, we did not use any tanks while spear fishing. This was one regulation that we all favored, as it minimized the chance of 'over-fishing' and depleting the fish stocks in and around Nassau. Robert Kennedy came up with a lobster that was gorgeous in both size and looks.

We were down about twenty feet or maybe a little more when I spied a lobster with the antennae jutting out from a cave-like hole at the bottom of a large coral reef. The reef was covered with various colors of coral, coral flowers and growth and was seemingly covered with hundreds of small and large fish dashing to and fro around the reef.

A 'gorgeous' lobster?' you might be thinking! How can anything as ugly as a lobster be anything but just plain ugly and in a sense fearsome looking! Fearsome is a good word to describe a lobster when you view it through a mask as you are snorkeling. They look awesome as they are backed into a hole in the coral with only their antennae and partial facial features staring out at you.

As I approached the lobster to get a good shot at it all of a sudden I felt a stinging sensation in my right leg just above the ankle. This got my immediate attention and I turned to look down at my leg to determine the cause of the pain and in so doing, when looking behind,

The Final Dive

I spotted Bobby signaling to me with his arm and hand waving as he pointed off to my left side. I swung my head over to the left and then I saw it. A monster of a lobster staring out from the coral reef and looking as if it was daring either of us to get any closer. Bobby signaled me once again by tapping my ankle with his spear. I could see his hand signals quite clearly as he pointed to his chest, then pointed to the spear he was holding and then he pointed towards the lobster. I got the message instantly and signaled for us to go to the surface. We both gave a push and covered the twenty feet or so to the surface in about 30 seconds.

We removed the snorkels from out of our mouths and between heavy breathing Bobby said "Did you see the size of that Lobster?" I answered, between breaths, "Bobby I sure did." I then asked him what happened that made him try to get my attention by tapping me on the ankle with his spear. He replied with a sly but humorous grin on his face; "I didn't want you to get that monster, I wanted to get myself...what a trophy." "Let's do it!" I shot back and into our mouths went our snorkels and with a strong dive and a strong push with our flippers we were on our way back down for the "Trophy" as Bobby called it.

Swimming side by side we approached the lobster and Bobby really surprised me as he lifted the spear, pulling it through the bamboo he held and fitting the rear of the spear into the metal cup attached with surgical rubber. Dead aim and a dead lobster....I reached down, grabbed it by the antennae and with a successful nod of our heads we were on our way to the surface. We broke surface and removing snorkels from our mouths we congratulated one another on a fine hunting trip and how we were going to really enjoy dinner. Laughter and joking with humorous comments we approached the boat and tossing the lobster inside as we climbed back into the boat we were greeted by Gardner and one other diver with "Wow" and "Amazing" and "What a catch." "Wait until the others return and see this monster."

The coral reefs are far too beautiful for me to even attempt to adequately describe. The whole underwater scene is enchanting, awesome, awe-inspiring, overpowering, irresistible, and it is like a magnet as it draws you to itself. Do I recommend snorkeling in the Bahamas? You bet I do. I wish everyone could at least, once in their lifetime, snorkel, dive, or spear fish in the Bahamas, or, as I have, in the Virgin Islands, Puerto Rico, Hawaii and California. You think going to Disneyland is an experience? Well, it is but compared to the experience of a spear fishing or snorkeling trip, Disneyland is a close second best, in my opinion.

High noon, lobster boiling in a pot, fresh Bloody Mary's in coffee cups all around with the exception of the two on-duty security people. Laughter and the sharing of experiences as each one of us told 'our' version of what we had encountered, how we dealt with it and the final outcome.

The Final Dive

There was the shark story from one, the sighting of a four hundred pound grouper (although rare still very possible in these waters) from another. The lobster tails, having been boiled to perfection in about twenty minutes, were served. Sam, a chef par excellence, added just the right amount of ingredients to the lobster mix to serve an absolute banquet of lobster. He shared some of the recipes but not all of it. When pushed, he admitted that the dish consisted of chopped onions, butter, with a layer of cheese on top. There were a few other touches that Sam deemed 'his secret' and 'his alone'. And when he added some black- eyed peas and rice as a side on the same plate with the lobster, the food gods in heaven applauded. After the meal and about a one hour rest we prepared for an afternoon dive. Enthusiasm ran high and with snorkeling gear on we entered the water one more time. I found myself paired up with James, one of the security folks assigned to Mr. Kennedy. He was an excellent diver and it was obvious that he was accustomed to diving; he was agile and apparently quite skilled, in my estimation. I was, in about an hour's time, going to find out just how good he really was as we encountered one heck of a large barracuda. James and I scoped out some reefs near the surface of the water and keeping an eye out for a grouper for dinner or another lobster. We came upon a ship wreck lying on its side, in about fifteen feet of water…easy to reach for someone who was snorkeling and not SCUBA diving. I remember someone earlier on, while we were on deck, asking what SCUBA stood for and I had told her it was an acronym for "Self-Contained Underwater Breathing Apparatus.

James signaled that he wanted to go down and check out the wreck. I nodded in agreement and we both headed down in a straight dive propelling ourselves with our flippers. Two minutes on the wreck and we headed back to the surface. We removed our snorkels and chatted for a while about the wreck and then taking a deep breath we headed back down. Then it happened….my heart jumped as I spotted a huge four or five foot barracuda heading right toward us just a few hundred yards away. I hit the wreck with my spear and got James' attention. Signaling him to head up he followed me to the surface. I said, "James there is one huge barracuda down there that seems interested in us." James spoke up, "What's the plan?" he asked. I explained that it would be much wiser to keep an eye on the barracuda than just swim away. "Just follow my example, I explained and keep a sharp watch on that fish." Barracuda can be very, very dangerous to swimmers and particularly to someone snorkeling as barracuda are aware, instantly, of a kill that a person spearfishing might be carrying. A barracuda can reach lengths of up to more than six feet, they are scavengers and sometimes can mistake a snorkeler for a large predator. They follow the snorkeler hoping, as I mention above, to eat the remains of their catch. They have very prominent sharp-edged teeth, are snake like in appearance and are downright scary to encounter, especially if you have a fish on the end of your spear.

I signaled to James and I flipped over on my back I was near the surface with my snorkel out of the water for breathing and my mask just under the surface. I kept low in the water and I could see down the length of my body, through the mask I was wearing, and past my toes. I watched as the barracuda took up a position about forty or fifty feet past my flippers and he started to swim back and forth parallel to James and I but followed us all the way back to the boat. I had told James to keep his spear at the ready at all times and to swim in a calm manner. As we approached the boat the activity of the other swimmers and the noise emanating from the boat deck stopped the advance of the barracuda and he left the area. Much to the relief of James and myself. I had been through similar situations after years of diving and snorkeling so I felt relatively safe…unfortunately this was James first encounter with a predator, and as James put it, "with such enormous teeth and so ferocious looking." The talk about that experience went on for some time and ended only after Gardner docked the boat and we went ashore.

What a day this had been, total enjoyment. We loaded up the van and headed back out to Lyford Cay. Lots more laughter and story-telling. It was obvious by the mood that everyone had a great time, and for that I was grateful.

We drove into Lyford Cay, and as I pulled to a stop in front of the Kennedy house Robert asked, "Hey, Terry, how about joining us for a trip into Nassau tonight; you could show us some of the sights?"

"Is he kidding?" I thought to myself, "Wow! What an opportunity, what a privilege!" I am in total awe of the man and he talks to me as if he has known me his whole life. "Of course, I would be honored; what time would you like me to pick you up?" "How about seven o'clock?" interjected Billings, "we can have dinner at your favorite spot; how does that sound to you, Robert?"

Mr. Kennedy looked pensive for a minute then said "Great." "I'll be here at seven", I replied. Climbing back into the van, I was off with a happy heart and a song on my lips...humming 'This is my island in the Sun", a beautiful Island song made popular in 1957 by Harry Belafonte and sung throughout all the islands in the sun, including Nassau.

I called the Nassau Yacht Club Hotel, located directly across from the Nassau Yacht harbor, and made reservations. I didn't tell them who the honored guest was going to be.

We arrived at 7:30 pm and sat down to a scrumptious meal of lobster salad Bahamian style. Some of the ingredients that were added to the salad were lemon juice, salt, with mixed salad greens and whatever else that incredibly talented cook put in. The main dish was baked grouper topped with bread crumbs and cheese added to form a crust on the grouper, plus whatever else the cook deemed necessary to produce one of the finest dishes I had ever eaten. Robert and the rest of the gang marveled at the taste and there was agreement all around that eating in the Bahamas was in itself a real treat.

Mr. Kennedy kept a low profile and dressed in a manner that allowed him to just 'fit in'. The conversation during dinner was pleasant, light-hearted and amiable. Initially, not one person in the dining room realized that Robert Kennedy, possibly the next president of the United States, was sitting right there alongside them enjoying dinner just as they were.

When dinner was over we were off to Peanuts Taylor's 'Drumbeat Club' to enjoy some good down to earth Bahamian music. To a Bahamian, music is the most central element in his or her life, with traditional Junkanoo and goombay leading the list. Bahamians are a nation of music makers and music lovers.

Music in the Bahamas shows a marked influence from music around the world. Calypso, Latin rhythms from Cuba and Mexico, including contemporary music from the United States, all leave an indelible mark in Bahamian music.

Peanuts Taylor himself was one of the first Bahamian entertainers to come to international attention. Peanuts was born John Berkley Taylor. The nickname 'Peanuts' came about when Peanuts challenged renowned dancer

Paul Meeres, claiming he (Peanuts) could dance better than the famed star, to which Meeres replied "Why you're nothing but a peanut." The nickname stuck and lasted a lifetime.

Peanuts enjoys the distinction of being the first 'Musical Ambassador of the Bahamas' touring the globe and performing on top American televisions shows such as Johnny Carson and Ed Sullivan.

I left the van behind and was driving a 1966 Chevrolet light blue convertible as we headed for Peanuts Taylor's 'Drumbeat Club' located just 'Over the Hill' where the local entertainment centers were located. Due to the nature of the business I was in I had different vehicles at my disposal, and hence I could switch vehicles as the need dictated. As we drove to the club I continued to give my guests more history of Peanuts Taylor. Continuing my dialogue, I explained that Peanuts was the first person ever to do 'The Limbo' on national television; this was in 1957. He then toured Bermuda and California where he opened for such celebrities as Sammy Davis Junior, The Mills Brothers, and Nat King Cole.

Peanuts' magic with drums was heralded throughout the music and night club world. He played five drums of various sizes at one time while alternating with one elbow on the goatskin drums. He was an actual marvel to watch. Peanuts Taylor was a major part of the Bahamian music world since 1939, and when he returned to the Bahamas, after his tour, he built the

Drumbeat Club and was the feature entertainment. I was absolutely positive that all my guests were in for the treat of their life, and I wasn't disappointed and neither were they.

Peanuts Taylor drummed as he had never drummed before, and while he entertained everyone in the place we, at our table, engaged in good natured banter and sharing of more stories about the day's diving excursion. The only difference with story-telling now as opposed to the time immediately after the dive is that we were having a few drinks and that made all the stories longer, wider and filled with more hair-raising close calls with all types of denizens of the deep, most of which were well-imagined. The rum and coke and whatever everyone, except the two FBI types, was drinking flowed liberally, and in a short while we were happy, relaxed and enjoying the good time. No one in the party drank too much. Just enough to make the evening light, fun and enjoyable.

There were a few folks that recognized Robert, and a couple that had the courage to ask for an autograph or a photograph with him. Robert was a gentleman at all times and was very agreeable and accommodating to all. He seemed to be interested in the welfare of the locals and pursued this interest by asking many questions.

At one point Robert asked me if it would be possible to have Peanuts join us. I left the table and sought out Peanuts on one of his breaks. I explained that I was with Robert Kennedy and that Robert would like him to join us for a drink if he was able to.

Peanuts, like Robert, a gentleman and very courteous, was agreeable and joined us for a drink and some conversation. He sat next to me and directly across from Robert. As it was intermission time the music was low and most of the folks were dancing. Robert thanked Peanuts for the entertainment and expressed his gratitude for the magnificent performance.

Then the two of them engaged in some pretty serious conversation about the islands, the cost of living, the job market and how the people of the Bahamas sustained themselves. Peanuts assured Robert that the folks in the Bahamas could always benefit from more income but, on the whole, were pretty happy people.

Salaries were low, Peanuts was explaining, and at this point Mr. Kennedy asked me how comfortable a living was I able to enjoy in the Bahamas while earning a Stateside (US) salary.

I offered that I did quite well and enjoyed a very comfortable lifestyle with my family, but that the British style of employing people in other countries unfortunately resulted from the fact that the British thought that every place outside their own country was just a colony and as such they really didn't need to step up to the plate and generously share the wealth. Only a smile appeared on Robert's face, and when I looked at Peanuts he too was smiling. Sometimes agreement can be revealed in a most enchanting and subtle way without saying a word.

The times were good, the partying was fun and there was no shortage of people coming by our table as Robert was getting recognized by more and more people. He was never uncomfortable, and wished everyone well. Whenever someone had a question to ask he gave that person rapt attention. His answers were always cordial and brief. Sometimes when someone was going on a little too long and he sensed what the ultimate question might be he just politely cut in and answered the unasked question with courtesy.

Naturally, because of all the stories I had heard about the infamous womanizing that was attached to all the Kennedy males, I was keenly aware of Robert's reaction when the young ladies approached. I watched a man that kept a polite and respectful distance from them all. He never personally engaged any of them in conversation but he would always give them the same respectful answers that he gave everyone else. I was reminded also about how often he mentioned his wife, Ethel, and the children. He would, at the drop of a hat, talk about his family. He discussed their achievements with the same pride that one would find in any father that loved his children. He was so darn proud of them all, and I can attest to the fact that when he spoke of Ethel his face lit up and there was always a smile when her name was mentioned.

Time to go, it was getting late and there were a few yawns amongst us. The only ones that appeared totally alert to every little detail were Rodney and James, the two FBI types that were there. They just enjoyed everything that we were enjoying. The difference was that they were keenly alert to everything that was going on. I was to see in just a few minutes, when we stepped outside the entrance to the club to retrieve my car, just how quickly these two could react and take charge of what could have been a volatile situation.

Rodney held the door open and James walked out first, and as soon as James was out the door Rodney stepped back inside and was at Robert's back. I only heard one word and then there was commotion. I could not make out what the word was but it came from James.

I turned to look at Robert Kennedy and I noticed that Rodney was now in front of him and was looking over Robert's shoulder to cover Robert's back to see if there was any approaching danger.

Meanwhile, James had leapt from the step at the entrance toward a hedge that was directly in front of us. The hedge ran alongside the roadway with a break in the hedge for a foot path. I heard a scream, and Rodney was standing holding the wrist of a female. She was about twenty five years old, had short black hair and was wearing a very nice and what appeared to be expensive dress. In her right hand, the one Rodney was holding, was a black object, which turned out to be a camera. There were a few minutes of conversation between the two security men and being the experts that these two were they quickly realized that there was no danger.

The girl had seen Robert inside the club and wanted to get a picture of him exiting the club with the club name in the background. Her intentions, it was discovered, were not honorable and having just a picture of Robert Kennedy was not her only goal. A picture of Robert Kennedy, possibly the next President of the United States, emerging from a night club in the Bahamas in the wee hours of the morning could have earned her some dubious fame and quite a few dollars.

The excitement over, we walked to my car and settled ourselves in for the ride back to Lyford Cay. "Everyone buckled up?" I asked. Affirmative answers all around, and as I drove the vehicle out of the parking lot onto the road I glanced back and noticed that my two new friends, James and Rodney, were not buckled up. After the excitement of the past few minutes I understood with much more clarity just why they were not. We drove in silence for quite a while and then the faithful Mr. Billings calmly mentioned "I had a great time". We all agreed and started to make plans for the next diving trip, which was to take place on the afternoon of the following day. Looking at my watch I noticed that the 'following day' was already part of our lives... it was almost three o'clock in the morning.

After dropping everyone off at 'The Cottage' at Lyford Cay I headed to the other side of the Island and my own home. The drive back, to the other end of the Island, where we had a rented house, was more than pleasant. There was a full moon, the palm trees held my attention as the moonbeams danced off the shiny leaves. I was looking forward to seeing my wife, Maureen, and our two boys, Shawn and Michael.

My heart was beating fast from the day and the night activities. I was overwhelmed with a feeling of excitement and sheer joy. What a story to tell my wife and kids, what a story one day to tell my grandchildren. Life was good for me, but unfortunately it was not as good for Maureen and the kids. I'll get into that a little later on. I saw a parking spot down by the beach and I pulled into it.

I took out a cigarette and lit up. My mind was reeling, I tilted my seat back a little, then resting my head, I thought of the day's activities. Those two security types impressed me to no end. Fast, intelligent and so aware of everything that was going on.

What was it Billings had said the day before? "Terry, you don't really think that we would go fishing with you without checking on you first, do you?" It was more a statement than a question. I knew he was telling me the truth because he mentioned that they knew I was the president of the Nassau Sea Hunters and he had even mentioned the incident at the swimming pool that had made the local paper.

I started to reflect on that incident and my mind wandered back to the Shamrock Cottages and 'The Incident at the Swimming Pool.'

The year was 1965, just a little over a year prior to my outing with Mr. Kennedy, that the incident at the swimming pool had taken place. I remembered it as I took another puff on my cigarette and blew the smoke off into the Bahamian night, I thought back to my first encounter with 'the swimming pool' ....

......I was remembering driving past the ancient Montague Beach Hotel located on the east end of the Island and then headed up a long narrow street shaded by large overgrown trees whose branches reach across the road high overhead. These branches form a canopy that effectively blocks out the torturous skin-burning rays of the sun. All at once I found myself amidst a cluster of small cottages, whose name almost denies one the pleasure of being in the Bahamas. This cluster of cottages is known as 'Shamrock Cottages'. How this gathering of small one bedroom tourist accommodations got its name is anyone's guess. My own recollection is that they were once owned by a displaced Irishman who came to these islands to make his fortune in rum-running to the shores of the United States during Prohibition, much as some early American politicians and others made their fortunes. Unfortunately for the Irishman, his own product got the better of him, or maybe got the worst of him depending on how one looks upon such a careless statement.

Over the years he had realized his dream of making a fortune many times. Then one morning he awoke to find that his fortune was once again squandered, but this morning was to be vastly different. This pathetic man made a decision, a determined decision to be a legend in his own time rather than a legend in his own mind as had been the case for years.

He had another brilliant idea as to how this was to come about. He was rapidly losing all his friends, and to keep the ones he had he took the last of his money and built what became 'Shamrock Cottages'. And so it came to pass, that in a circle which had been cleared of trees only to the extent that a clearing large enough for each cottage should be made, the wee cottages were built. Seven of them spaced far enough apart to ensure privacy, forming a complete circle with a rather large swimming pool in the center. The front door of each cottage was not more than thirty feet from the edge of the pool. Ah, Paradise found at last, or so hoped this rugged little Irishman.

Unfortunately, so the story goes, the day after his project was completed he was found sitting at the table in his kitchen with a bottle of whiskey, almost empty standing upright as if at attention, on the table in front of him.

A half-filled glass of the stuff, seemingly at half-mast, was clasped in a tight clenched fist and he was stone cold dead. The cottages sold at auction.

Grinding out my cigarette in the car's ashtray, I reached into the glove compartment of the vehicle and took out a flask of rum. After a long swallow I put the flask in my jacket pocket. Stepping away from the car, I lit another cigarette and made myself comfortable sitting on the stump of a fallen tree. Basking in the pool of moonlight that lit up the early morning night I continued to think about the swimming pool incident and the things that had transpired since that time.

I had been living at Shamrock Cottages for about a year when we were early into 1965 never realizing the massive change that was to take place before another year was ended. An event of historic proportions was in the making and I would know one of the key players in a more or less intimate way. I was to have the pleasure and sad misfortune of being one of the last persons to spend a vacation with the then Senator Robert Kennedy just prior to his assassination.

My business relationships and social relationships, most important to my way of thinking at the time, were the relationships that were brought about and cemented by water sports. Deep sea fishing, underwater photography, treasure hunting, and spear fishing. The latter was my first love! I can remember spending days out on a clear glass smooth ocean in my 28 ft. weekender sometimes referred to as a cabin cruiser. Diving from early light until I was too exhausted to dive anymore or darkness overtook us. On more than one occasion our dives were cut short by the presence of sharks.

From Montreal up in Canada to the California coast; from Los Angeles to Saint Thomas in the Virgin Islands, where I first learned to dive; to Puerto Rico and then on to my present home in the Bahamas. With the first sighting of the clear blue and emerald green waters I was drawn to them as metal is drawn to a magnet. My destiny was sealed. That same destiny that I always believed was mine was not; it belonged to the beauty that captured me. That same destiny that drove me from the Virgin Islands to the beautiful Bahamas.

The swimming pool incident started to fill my mind again with the happenings of that day as I sat on this old tree stump. I had a vivid vision of 'Shamrock Cottages' on, as usual, another hot and sticky day. A burning sun overhead, a cloudless sky, palm trees climbing to the sky without a whisper of a breeze to stir those magnificent branches. I took another long swallow out of that rum bottle and, letting out a sigh that only a stirred memory can bring, I began to think of the past and the incident at the swimming pool.

The "Common Folks" of the cottages, as they were affectionately known, were keeping to the indoors to take advantage of the air-conditioning. Just four of us sitting around the pool, Lonnie, a mechanic for Bahamas Airlines, his wife, Angelica, their infant son, Harold, and me.

All the diving for treasure, the diving on wrecks, the formal dinners with black tie and cummerbund, the business of running a business, all of this pales and slips into a hazy background as I remember 'The Incident at the swimming pool."

I was sitting at one end of the pool, the deep end, which is about eight feet deep, then slanting to a depth of about eleven feet at the center and further slanting to about four feet deep at the shallow end.

Lonnie was sitting at the other end with his feet resting on the semi-circular steps that were just under the surface of the water. I remembered counting the steps; there were three of them, the top one being about ten inches underwater, the next one down about twenty-two inches and the third step just a few inches off the bottom.

Angelica, Lonnie's wife, was sitting off to the side, a few feet from her cottage door at one of those big round tables with a large umbrella sticking out of the center of the table to shade her from the sun. She was writing a letter back home to her parents and to her in-laws who lived in England.

Lonnie and Angelica had come to the Bahamas to seek a better life, and a better life it was for the both of them. They loved Nassau, the great days of no rain, the bringing up of Harold away from the influence of overwhelming but all-too-busy grandparents. Harold was sitting beside his father at the other end of the pool with his feet dangling in the water. Every once in a while he would squeal with delight as the coolness splashed up around him. Remembering back, I thought to myself that Harold was due for a full flotation device as he was starting to experiment with adventure.

I was working on some diving gear I had just purchased and at the same time I was talking to Lonnie at the other end of the pool. I held up a new regulator which was one of the first single hose regulators that I owned, and I was telling Lonnie that I was pretty happy with the way it performed. Lonnie was straining to see what I was pointing to as I explained a particular function to him. My attention was diverted from the other end of the pool for what seemed a fraction of a second, and when I looked back I noticed that Harold had left the pool. I looked over to where his mother was sitting, expecting to see him there. No Harold. I scanned the short space between the pool and the table where she was writing. No Harold. I thought to myself, 'Now where has that kid gone?'

Something caught my eye in the pool, a movement, ever so slight on the second step down right beneath Lonnie's feet. "Lonnie!" I yelled as I stood up and took a long body spread out dive into the water stretching my body out as far as it would go. "Lonnie", I yelled again as my body hit the water. I pushed and strained with all my might underwater as I tried to see the other end of the pool. Harold had slipped into the water and was lying on the second step. No movement, no thrashing, just stillness. Lonnie had no idea what had happened, because I'd taken his attention away for a few seconds with my yelling about the new equipment.

He heard me yell at the same time he saw me hit the water. Instead of looking down at his feet he was watching my progress through the water just under the surface.

Only a few more feet to go. Thank God I was a powerful swimmer, having trained myself to be able to dive to a depth of thirty-five feet while spear fishing. This may not sound too unusual, except that when I was spear fishing I never used SCUBA gear, it was all free diving.

I can hold my breath for three minutes at a time and my lungs and arms were in great shape. As I stretched out reaching for the other end of the pool I had an instant flashback to some of the training that members of our spear fishing club took in order to improve ourselves for when we had contests with other clubs.

Winning became a very serious matter. I had been president of our club, 'The Nassau Sea Hunters', and always insisted on very rigorous training sessions. One part of the training consisted of lying on my back in the pool and having my ankles tied together. Then floating on my back I would swim around the perimeter of the pool using my arms and dragging my body as a dead weight. During this exercise I used only the upper part of my body, the arms, shoulders and back muscles. This exercise is designed to strengthen all of the upper body and in particular the lungs.

In one last lunge I had Harold in my arms, and with the swiftness that still amazes me to this day I was up and out of the water. Lonnie was beside me, Harold was slightly blue around the mouth. Angelica, with a shriek, was bounding across the grass towards us. "Dammit, Harold" I cried to myself, "Don't die on me". Angelica was crying, Lonnie was standing staring. Harold was so still, so limp in my arms. I turned him over and cradled him in the crook of my left arm, and as he lay there I took the flat of my hand and smashed him on the back. I flipped him over and noticed that there was no change; in fact he appeared to be a little more blue around the mouth. I reached down and put the heel of my right hand into the middle of Harold's little tummy just below the ribs. Angelica was getting hysterical. "Do something" she screamed. Lonnie was standing rigid, in shock. I pushed down into that little tummy, a trickle of water slipped out from between the baby's lips. I pushed down again, but this time with a forceful thrust and a thump.

All at once a gusher of water spewed forth out of that little mouth, another push, more water, a scream ... It wasn't Angelica this time, it was Harold. Coughing, and gagging, spitting out water with bile. Then all at once it was over. Harold looked up and through small coughs he cried out, in a small barely audible voice, the word that has been shouted around the world by babies and grown men and women alike, "Mama." Angelica reached out and took Harold from me. I looked across at Lonnie and through the tears I heard him say, "Thank you, God."

No, I guess I never will forget the 'Swimming Pool Incident'. I tossed the remains of the cigarette into the incoming tide, and standing up I stretched and returned to my car. On the way to the car I finished off the little rum that remained in the flask and headed home to the most wonderful wife and friend that a man could be blessed with. I was soon to learn that too much alcohol makes for a bad relationship and turns decent people into useless and lousy husbands ... a lesson learned by me but unfortunately a lesson learned too late.

The next day came much too soon and the sunlight in the bedroom almost blinded me. I swallowed a couple of Tylenol to deal with my now throbbing head. Out of the house and into my car; it was high noon and I was on my way out to Lyford Cay to pick up my diving buddies, Robert, Billings, James and Rodney.

My good friend Sam Cancilla was riding along with me, we were as excited as two kids at Christmas time and the chatter was nonstop.

Sam and I talked about some of the things that we do in Nassau to keep busy and to enjoy as two buddies. Our wives understood (at least I think they did) that we just needed to get out and get doing things. Sam's wife, Terri, was almost identical in personality, gentleness, loving and caring as my wife, Maureen, inasmuch as they gave us plenty of free time to enjoy our favorite sports. Sam and I were young, healthy and full of spit. One of our favorite pastimes was going to the city dump on a Saturday morning to shoot rats.

We each owned a few pistols and a couple of rifles. My rat-shooting gun was a Browning semi-automatic twenty-two-caliber target pistol.

Sam was from Ontario and had a very successful career as one-half of a singing, guitar playing duo called 'The Talismen'. They were very popular in the '70's and were based in Florida. The other half of the duo was Michael Smith, who is still out on the circuit singing and playing his guitar. He is very popular and still in demand. When Sam moved to Nassau with his wife, Teri, and their two children, Dominick and Shauna, he continued to wow the folks at the local clubs with the mellow and rich sound of his voice.

Sam and I met up at a local amateur group of performers called 'The Nassau Amateur Operatic Society.' Operatic we were not. We did shows such as 'South Pacific' and the like. Once, the whole cast sang and entertained for the Duke of Edinburgh's visit to Nassau. I am not sure if the Duke was impressed, but we got rave reviews anyhow. As for me, I was not a singer but did bit parts in the performances. My introduction was via my wife, Maureen, who was and still is a very fine and talented singer. She is also a comedienne and still thrills many with her quick wit and sense of humor. She was a starlet in her own right whenever she took to the stage.

As we continued our drive out to Lyford Cay this fine sunny day Sam and I talked a lot about Nassau and living here. The ocean is the prevailing feature of the Bahamas with the offshore being rimmed by some of the greatest barrier reefs in the world. The ocean and the trailing seven hundred islands that make up the Bahamas are a geographical wonder and incredible attraction and inspiration. Painters, boat builders, sailors, fishermen and divers all agree that without the ocean the Bahamas would probably lose its underlying principle and validation of beauty, diving, and all hosted by some of the loveliest and friendly people in the world.

The water ranges from a beautiful aqua to an ever-deepening sapphire; the colors change as the sun glides across the sky with the occasional dip to kiss the waters and the people of the Bahamas. Although only an hour's flight from Florida, its glamorous, colorful and exotic appeal makes one feel like they are in some foreign and alien land that was created personally by the hand of God.

It is shrouded in mysterious folk tales, and not so openly discussed are the 'in the dead of night happenings' like the disappearance and supposed murder of the Canadian entrepreneur, Oakes. The Bahamian people, as I have mentioned before, are the most wonderful, honest and friendly folks that can be found anywhere. In days gone by you could take a walk, at any time of the night, across a secluded beach, and the only company you would have would be the imprint left by your feet in the soft warm sand.

As we drove along, Sam and I started talking about the island's most famous and notorious murder case, the Sir Harry Oakes case. It is never discussed amongst locals on the Island and is definitely a taboo subject in any public discussions. Intrigue, after all these years, still surrounds the case. "So, Sam", I was asking, "what is your opinion on this whole Oakes thing?"

"Well, Terry", Sam started, and I knew I was in for an education concerning this murder, because Sam was also a Private Detective and had worked on some intriguing cases in Nassau for some very well-established American Government agencies. I had accompanied Sam on a few cases, as a sort of minor helper but more as an interested 'onlooker.'

"As you know, Terry, Oakes was a multi-millionaire from Canada whose life came to a quick and probably painful end in July of 1943 out there at his Nassau estate. His head was shattered by repeated blows and his body was partially destroyed by fire. Oakes' good friend Harold Christie was asleep in an adjoining room and claimed he never heard a sound. It is said that what followed was one of the most incompetent cases of police work ever witnessed. Oakes' son-in-law was arrested on suspicion of murder but was found not guilty in just less than two hours.

"The case was never reopened". Sam continued, "This is one of the most interesting and readable murder cases and has garnered attention around the world. It is still talked about today but hardly ever discussed in Nassau", Sam concluded as we pulled into the Lyford Cay Estates.

Back on board Gardner Young's charter boat we prepared once again to 'get at it'. Excitement ran high and we were all anxiously waiting to see what we would encounter once we hit the water. There was talk of sharks being sighted in the area and Gardner reminded us to be ever watchful and if a shark was sighted just to head back to the boat. One person heading back would be a signal to all that something might be wrong. The instructions completed, our anxiety rate climbed a little. Mine did even though I have been diving in these and other shark- inhabited waters for years. I have seen my share of sharks and there have been a few close encounters, they are rare but it does happen. The closest I ever came to what might be considered dangerous was when a shark had made a pass at me. Once circled, I made my way to my boat and climbed out of the water, my diving buddies did the same and we headed for another diving spot. There were other encounters over the years but all ended well.

Into the water we went, spear fishing equipment at the ready. We were going to give our guests a lesson in spear fishing and the outcome was that we were going to barbecue our catch that evening at Lyford Cay. Spear fishing in the Bahamas was disallowed recently within one mile from the island but in the old days we could spear fish right off shore. Spear fishing then as now was not allowed with SCUBA tanks or arbalets. An arbalet is a spear gun that is powered by a heavy surgical rubber band or mechanism that can be locked in place and has a trigger release. The only spear fishing equipment allowed in Bahamian waters without a permit, at the time of our dive, was called a 'Hawaiian Sling'.

Rubber Powered Arbalet Spear Gun

Briefly described, a Hawaiian sling is comprised of a piece of bamboo approximately six or eight inches in length with a piece of surgical rubber with a small metal cup to hold the spear attached to the center of the rubber. The surgical rubber was affixed to the bamboo by way of heavy cord or string adhered and sealed with fiberglass resin or some such adherent.

Hawaiian Sling

The spear was then inserted through the center of the bamboo, where a hole existed and snugly fit into the metal cup. The sling was then drawn back much like the string on a bow if you were shooting arrows. The bamboo was held in the left hand and the rubber and spear were drawn back by the right hand. When a fish was in your sights you just drew back on the surgical rubber that was attached to the bamboo and released the spear.

My good buddy Sam came up with the first and biggest fish, a really big and impressive grouper. This didn't surprise me, as Sam is one of the best spear fishermen that I have ever had the pleasure of watching during a dive. He has an incredible sixth sense when in the water. It is uncanny how he is able to know just where to be at the right moment to spear the big ones.

Next came La Moyne Billings with a huge lobster followed by James with a near record size conch shell. Sam, as the designated cook would show us all how to release the meat from the conch shell. Now we all knew that a meal with a king-sized taste and king-sized proportions was awaiting us that evening.

As we toasted our success with the usual Bloody Marys' made up of vodka and tomato or V8 juice with added ingredients like hot Louisiana sauce or other ingredients added and mixed to taste, we raised our glasses and/or cups and then the tales began to fly. The size of the one that got away, including the imagined enormous fight that ensured prior to its flight from the end of someone's spear. The stories were good-natured and there was congeniality all around.

Leaving the charter boat, Sam and I drove our guests back to Lyford Cay and made arrangements to be back for the barbeque later that evening. Sam, because of his reputation as a seasoned and professional cook, particularly of exotic foods, was elected unanimously to prepare and do the cooking. Sam agreed, and we all looked forward to a great evening at Lyford Cay.

It was about ten o'clock and there was a full and beautiful golden moon shining a golden path across the ocean that greeted me on the beach, where I found myself walking, just a few yards from the house that Bobby and his guests were staying in. After excusing myself from the group. The dinner went well, and Sam, true to his word, barbequed up one of the finest fish barbeques that I have ever had. There was absolutely no difference of opinion from any of the others.

The conversations were congenial and informative, peppered throughout with gales of laughter as one or the other of us related the specifics of his engagement with a fish or some coral during the afternoon diving trip. After I expressed my desire to take a walk down by the beach and got the approval of all, I took off.

I have always loved the ocean at night and in the early morning. A full moon, cast as straight as an arrow, beams of golden yellow across the ocean with what appeared to be a beginning on the horizon and ending at the shoreline, then moving silently and gently across the well-manicured lawns and settling in the palm trees.

I heard footsteps behind me and I turned to find Bobby catching up with me. "Is this incredibly beautiful, or what?" he spoke as he joined me. "You know what, Bobby, "I have seen a thousand moons like this on a thousand nights on a thousand beaches on many beautiful islands and on many beautiful lakes, but I am always amazed at the absolute beauty of it all. I never tire of looking at these scenes and each time it is as if I am seeing them for the first time."

"I think I can understand what you are driving at", he replied. "It is probably the poet in you. I remember that you mentioned to me that your hobby was short-story writing, poetry and writing short letters to friends on various subjects. It is probably the romantic in you that keeps you ever-vigilant to nature and God's creation". "You mention God", I stated with a little surprise in my voice. "Are you implying that this is all 'God'- made?" "I sure am, Terry. You don't think this all came about by chance, do you? After all, man can't even make a blade of grass or design a flower with so much beauty and perfectly-arranged colors and design!" "I suppose that makes some sense", I replied. "I am a Catholic like you Bobby and I have never thought much about God's handiwork in creation. It is something that we didn't discuss very much at home".

"Terry, you need to take a few minutes out of your schedule and do a little research into your own reason for existence in relationship to an Almighty God. You might just find that your writing will take on another and possibly more exciting theme and dimension." Robert continued to talk and I continued to listen with great interest. "I usually don't get too much into religion, but there seems to be a sentiment in me that is wanting me to share these thoughts with you. You seem to be a very sensitive person Terry and I can't help but feel that a touch of a force outside of yourself in your writing will reveal a whole new path to you. It is something to think about, anyhow", he concluded and we walked in silence for a while.

I blurted out, "Robert, how come a man of your importance would take the time out to discuss these things with me or even spend a couple of days spear fishing? I don't run in your circles, and let me assure you I am deeply honored. My question is one of curiosity and I really hope I haven't offended you." "Not at all Terry." I am of the opinion that every human being has value and that every person has something to offer. I am not much different than you or anyone else. But by the plan of God I am who I am and I am where I am.

There is not much that I have done myself; I have just tried to follow the leading as my heart, my desires, and my goals, have led me. You may not understand this, Terry, but I am as much bewildered by why you would spend so much time making my day a day to remember." Bobby kept talking and I kept listening...intently.

"You have been, as has been Sam Cancilla, your buddy, cordial, friendly, and in my opinion not judgmental nor seeking any favors by your actions and considerations. You don't seem to want anything in return for your giving, other than to see everyone have a good time, and for that, we, Le Moyne Billings and I and the others, are grateful".

"Thanks, I responded, I appreciate those words and I want to assure you that your suggestion about my writing and creation and the possible influence on my writings is accepted with deep gratitude. I am an inquisitive person and I will follow up". Which I eventually did some years later, and found a whole new purpose to my life that I had never dreamed possible. So ended another day in the Bahamas. On parting, Sam and I were invited back to Lyford Cay for a brunch the next day. It would be a farewell 'Thank You' as Billings put it, to Sam and me for giving of ourselves to make their diving in the Bahamas so enjoyable.

At eleven o'clock, Sam and I showed up for brunch. It was more like a feast than a simple meal. Stories were shared about diving, about the beauty of the Bahamas and then we touched on political matters, religion, poverty and friendships. At one point, when, in the midst of the 'political' part of the conversation, the death of John Kennedy came up, there was a silence at that moment that was complicated, uneasy and extraordinarily noticeable. My first thought regarding the assassination was, did Lee Harvey Oswald act alone or was there a conspiracy? Bobby, with his keen sense of timing, remarked, "Yes, a sad and tragic thing to have happened and I guess we will never really know all the details".

That ended the short time of silence, and, immediately, Bobby, with hardly a pause, continued the conversation by asking Sam and me about the cost of living in the Bahamas and the availability of products from the United States and England. What a great and wonderful human being, I thought, as I watched his expression go from pain for an instant for the suffering of humanity to the reality of the here and now. A short while after that time with Kennedy, I received a Christmas card from his family, and he took time out to write me a personal letter of thanks for a good time diving, and mentioned that he looked forward to doing it again sometime in the future. As we all know, that was never to happen. I am grateful to have spent his last vacation, in the Bahamas, with him and to have come to know him as a very sensitive and worthwhile human being.

I did follow up on his previous suggestion regarding an 'Almighty God'. On April 30, 1975 I had an encounter with God on a street in Waikiki, where I was living at the time, and that encounter changed my life forever. Robert was right; I made a decision on Christmas day in 1974 that had a life changing impact on my life and on my writing. Life and the creation of life and why we are here took on a whole new meaning for me.

I was a success, I had a beautiful, dedicated wife and I had two lovely sons. But I also had my booze. My booze, which I refer to as "The snake" because it had its deadly fangs dug deep into my mind and my body.

The Snake was my master and I served my master well. I sinned when he told me to. I sinned every kind of sin that only an alcoholic can sin. I was a slave. I couldn't get out of the trap. My master 'the snake' was cunning, secretive, and selective and his only goal was to destroy me. I couldn't get free, I wanted to do right, to be a good father to my children and a good husband to my wife……..I was trapped and I couldn't get free…….

Briefly, a little background; I started washing cars for a large car rental company at the Montreal International Airport after I left the Canadian Navy for the simple reason that I would rather obey my master, alcohol, rather than the commands of my superior officers. A glib tongue and a really hard work ethic pushed me ahead in that company in a hurry. From car washer to the rental desk and from the rental desk to the leasing department where I became the leasing manager for this company for all of Canada.

Then off to the Bahamas, the Virgin Islands, Puerto Rico, California and Hawaii in a maze of successes in the car rental business. I was young and overheard a superior refer to me as "Their Golden boy." What a compliment and none of them knew of my drinking problem. I was president of a spear fishing club in the Bahamas.

I enjoyed all the pleasures that alcohol can deliver.... and I didn't want to drink...but I couldn't stop.

But I wanted to.

Alcohol is a horrible addiction that will, without hesitation, take you into multiple other addictions. Drugs follow easily so does pornography and sex addiction, the addiction of lying fits in very nicely and the list goes on and on.

One day I overheard a woman telling a friend that she had put a pill into her husband's glass of beer and the husband became so sick he had to be rushed to the hospital where he almost succumbed to the violent sickness that overtook him. The wife was sorry that she did it but, as she explained to her friend, "I was so sick and tired of his drinking that I was willing to try anything to get him to stop." I listened with rapt attention, "A pill that would make you sick if you took it and drank" I mused to myself. I must find out more about this little pill.

So I discovered Antibuse. It is a pill that will make you violently ill if you drink any alcohol after you have taken it. I went to see a doctor. He gave me a prescription for a month's supply. For two weeks you take a whole pill every day. For the next two weeks you take a half a pill a day and then a quarter of a pill every day after that. So I took the pills and they worked.

I was deathly afraid to touch any booze just because of the description the doctor gave me of the illness I would suffer if I did drink plus the description that I had overheard as the woman described how her husband had become so violently ill after he had unknowingly taken the pill.

I went for two months without a drink but the Christmas Holidays were coming on so I decided to drop the pill. If you stop taking it for three or four days it leaves your system and is ineffective when you drink. So now I could have it both ways. I could take the pill when I didn't want to drink but if a party or social event was coming up I could just stop taking the pills for three days and I could drink and party until I felt like going back on the pill. It worked. I stopped taking the pill. I drank Christmas away and then I drank New Year's away and then I just kept on drinking. Ah, the best laid plans of mice and men...!!!

But I didn't go back to the pill and sometime later I was once again desperate and sick and tired of drinking and another way for me to stop drinking was about to present itself and once again I would grasp at the opportunity as a drowning man would grasp at anything to keep afloat.

My desire was always to stop drinking but unfortunately the disease had me in its death grip. My desire to stop was so strong that along with taking the *antibuse*, as I mentioned earlier, I sought out a priest in the Bahamas and decided to try the religious route. I can remember when I was young that my folks talked often about so and so taking the 'pledge' by praying with a priest in order to stop drinking….so I decided to take the 'pledge'.

As I explained to the priest, at the local Catholic Church, about my desire to stop drinking he asked how long I wanted to stop drinking for? I explained that I wanted to stop completely for the rest of my life. He replied with "Why don't we try for thirty days first?" I agreed to that and I knelt in his office and he prayed a most magnificent and heartwarming prayer. I could feel his sincerity as he spoke to God on my behalf. I rose from my kneeling position, thanked him and with a spring in my step I was out in the sunshine… delivered…from the beast. That deliverance lasted 29 days and I was back at it again. But as you read on you will find that I, one day, found the answer to my drinking problem and that answer came in the form of one sentence spoken by one of the most influential men in the world at that time….Robert F. Kennedy.

The year was 1974. I had been an alcoholic for almost 24 years. Divorced and alone in a little city in Illinois, just another city in my life's travels. I was broken…I was broken hearted and broken in my spirit. I was alone and surrounded by pain.

The pain in my heart was so enormous that I knew that I would never be a whole person again no matter how long I lived. I was the loneliest man on earth surrounded by happy, smiling, busy people and no knew I existed. I had ruined my life entirely and there was no going back, no making amends, no starting over.

I got into my four door Pontiac and headed for California. That was where my family, my ex-wife and my two sons were and I was going to say goodbye and end it all. Death and the thought of no more pain made me even smile a little. In a few days it would be over and I would have trampled that snake into the ground and I would know freedom. And above all my dream of not drinking would come true.

Three days later and a box of "No Doze" (a caffeine pill) and what seemed like a thousand cups of coffee I arrived in California. I visited with my ex-wife and two children…how beautiful they were and still are I might add. Then off to my sister's place; it was Christmas day

1974. My ex-wife, my two wonderful sons including my sister, two brothers, and their children had gathered together for the Christmas festivities and everyone was happy. They welcomed me and I put on a face of joy as best I could. Good food, lots of it, coupled with guitar playing and the Christmas songs being sung made me sad about my mission and why I was there.

This would be my last Christmas on this earth.

My brother, Paddy, sometime in the afternoon when things were quieter, asked me to join him in a separate room from the others. He expressed how sorry he was to see me in the shape I was in and wished he could help me in some way. I explained that it was all over and there was no use in even discussing it. I had reached the end of my rope.

Paddy pulled a small pamphlet out of his pocket and handed it to me…."Here Terrence," Patrick spoke, "read this…just take a few minutes and think about the words you are about to read." I thanked him and he walked out of the room.

I paced the floor and read things that I had never heard of in my life before…things about God. Well I am not religious with the exception that when I was a young Catholic lad and served as an altar boy at mass I would sneak into the back room where the priest kept the Sunday wine and guzzle as much as I could. So looking at it from that perspective I guess I was kind of religious.

As I continued to read I didn't see any flash of light and there was no thunder from the sky…in fact nothing happened….but I liked what Patrick had given me to read and the thought of God and me starting over made my heart beat a little faster…starting over would not be a new experience for me as I had done that many, many times in my life. Starting over with God? Well that was something else altogether. And as I had on a few other occasions, I thought of Bobby and his words….."Terry, you need to take a few minutes out of your schedule and do a little research into your own reason for existence in relationship to an Almighty God."

Patrick entered the room and I asked him if this was true and he said "Yes it is, do you want to give it a try?" "Sure", I said, "why not, what have I got to lose?" Can you imagine me, the filthiest guy in the world starting over…it is just too wild." So I prayed and nothing happened…I was still standing in the room with Patrick and I was still Terrence…except for one little detail…..I kind of felt at peace inside. I had not felt that calmness for so many years. I liked what I now felt.

As you can see by reading this I did not commit suicide……instead I left a few days later for Hawaii. When I arrived in Hawaii I looked up an old friend who, along with his father, owned a thriving business manufacturing and selling Hawaiian tourist items, in particular they sold a "Hawaiian Dollar." This item was hot and an easy item for me to carry along with my other tourist items that I sold, as their representative, to retail stores on the Island.

I loved God and my love for Him became stronger every day. Unfortunately I also had a hate/love relationship with alcohol. I just couldn't stop drinking. In the evenings I would sit on my lanai and read the bible….a glass of vodka in one hand, a cigarette in the other while balancing the bible and reading.

I devoured every word, the more I read the more I wanted to know who God was, I wanted to know His son, Jesus, on a more personal basis…I also wanted to stop drinking and I also wanted to stop smoking the three packs a day that were killing me. But I couldn't stop, I just couldn't do it. I prayed to God every day, I got so drunk that I would fall asleep while begging God to deliver me from alcohol.

Waking up would find me sitting in my chair on my lanai with an empty booze bottle at my feet, a half burned cigarette sitting on the floor and my precious bible clasped to my chest, holding onto that bible like a drowning man would clasp on to a life jacket in the middle of the ocean.

Twice, I was delivered from alcohol and cigarettes…. or so I thought. I remember jumping out of my chair, shouting "Halleluiah, halleluiah I am delivered."

I rushed into the kitchen and pouring the three remaining bottles of booze down the sink and walking around praising God for my deliverance…three hours later I was back at the liquor store and returning home with my usual stock of three 40 Oz bottles of Vodka......It was all an incredibly painful experience and I was so darn defeated and disappointed. But the next day I was back sitting in my chair on my lanai... booze, cigarettes and bible.....I refused to give up I wanted to know God more than I wanted anything in my life. I believed I was forgiven I believed that the bible was the word of God and I believed that God would not lie to me or trick me...I needed to NOT give up.

I spent three months in this state...but I would not give up...I trusted God and I was completely convinced that what I was going through was for a specific reason even if I did not know what that reason was. I drank, I smoked, I read my bible, I fell asleep drunk but I got up in the morning and I prayed and I read my bible and I kept doing that until one day in April... actually it was April 30, and the year was 1975. The time...sure I remember that also...it was 4:35pm.

Walking home from my place of employment along Kalakaua Avenue I was in a happy mood. Something was different and I didn't know what it was...there was just something inside of me that felt right, clean and good. I walked past the theatre and I watched a few people buying tickets to see the afternoon show. I walked past a bar with tables outside under shady trees and I saw the people sitting, drinking, socializing and plenty of laughter. Passing by I waved to a few folks that I knew…for I had spent many an hour and many a dollar sitting in that same spot.

Watching the cars as they whizzed by I observed a taxi pull up to the curb and two people getting out and heading into the bar. I brushed against a young man who was hurrying down the street in my direction….. it was just another crowded, busy day on Kalakaua Avenue….except for one significant difference……… there was not a sound…it startled me at first….was I going deaf?

I strained by ears to hear something…a car motor, some conversation or laughter from the people under the trees drinking and laughing and talking. There was nothing…It was as though I was in a vacuum. I could see everything in a perfectly normal manner…but the silence was more that deafening, it was scary…I looked around to see if anyone else was reacting to this silence. But their faces showed no signs of anxiety or care. It was as if a huge glass enclosure had come around me blocking out all noise but allowing me to see everything that was going on. Now I was becoming terrified…sweat broke out on my face, my hands and my whole body.

Pausing right there in the middle of the sidewalk on Kalakaua avenue and looking up to heaven I spoke these words; "God don't you think it's about time?"

There was a fearful and strange moment of silence as my voice bounced back into my ears and then I heard it….a voice.

It was a strange voice, not loud or mellow or booming. No it was just a plain clear, clean and well-spoken voice and this is what that voice said to me in my vacuum glass enclosure…

"It is finished." That was all, one short sentence, clear and concise…"It Is Finished!"

All at once I had a vision of Bobby Kennedy and myself walking and talking and Bobby's last words to me; "Terry, you need to take a few minutes out of your schedule and do a little research into your own reason for existence in relationship to an Almighty God."

At four thirty five on April thirtieth in the year 1975 I was delivered from alcohol and cigarettes. That was, as of this writing, forty one years ago. From that instant when I heard the voice of God proclaim "It is finished" I have never had a desire to drink any alcohol nor smoke a cigarette. Also I had no withdrawals and no after effects. When God performs a miracle whether it is on Kalakaua Avenue in Hawaii or in your own back yard…it is, as God in Heaven said…."Finished."

Here was God's promise to me direct into my heart: "For God so loved the world that he gave his one and only Son, that whoever believes in him shall not perish but have eternal life." So I went ahead and jumped in. One day I hope to have an incredible journey into eternity with God. The choice was mine to make. Who knows, maybe one day Bobby and I might just sit right down on a cloud and chat about "The Final Dive?"

My life was changed by a simple suggestion from a not so simple man, a man of great depth concerned with not only those dear to him, but with the suffering of all human beings on the planet. I owe Mr. Kennedy a debt I will never be able to repay.

Robert Kennedy's letter and the pictures I have of our time vacationing together, hang on my office wall at home, and I never tire of looking at them and reflecting on that time in my life. Some are included in this book with the hope that they will bring a smile to your face and put some joy and a happy memory in your heart….I am glad to share them with you.

                                            Terrence Morrissey

"The purpose of life is to contribute in some way to making things better."

Robert F. Kennedy

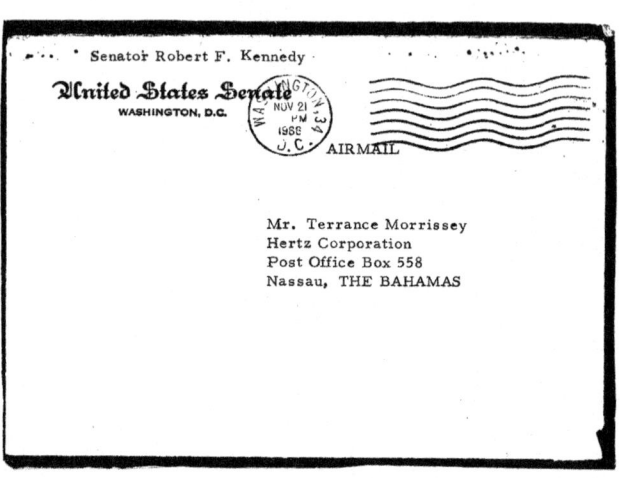

United States Senate
WASHINGTON, D.C.

November 18, 1966

Dear Mr. Morrissey:

I just wanted you to know how much I appreciated everything you did for us during our recent trip to Nassau. You were very thoughtful to give of your time -- and to be so helpful in so many ways.

I hope that someday Mrs. Kennedy and I shall have an opportunity to see you again. In the meantime, many thanks, and our warm regards,

Sincerely,

My Thanks to you
R. Kennedy

Robert F. Kennedy

Mr. Terrance Morrissey
Hertz Corporation
Post Office Box 558
Nassau, THE BAHAMAS

```
          United States Senate
            Washington, D.C.
```

November 18, 1966

Dear Mr. Greenbaum:

I wanted you to know what a great help Terrance Morrissey was to us during our recent visit to Nassau. He very thoughtfully gave of his time and in every instance went out of his way to be helpful. We were most grateful for his many kindnesses.

My thanks and best wishes,

                                           Sincerely,

                                           Robert F. Kennedy

Mr. Leon Greenbaum
Chairman
Hertz Corporation'
660 Madison Avenue
New York. New York

United States Senate
WASHINGTON, D.C.

November 18, 1966

Dear Mr. Greenbaum:

I wanted you to know what a great help Terrance Morrissey was to us during our recent visit to Nassau. He very thoughtfully gave of his time -- and in every instance went out of his way to be helpful. We were most grateful for his many kindnesses.

My thanks and best wishes,

Sincerely,

Robert F. Kennedy

Mr. Leon Greenbaum
Chairman
Hertz Corporation
660 Madison Avenue
New York, New York

CPSIA information can be obtained
at www.ICGtesting.com
Printed in the USA
LVOW04s2102150916
504735LV00011B/19/P